OBAMACARE 2014 - What Really Needs to Happen

Dr. Randy White

Copyright © 2014 Dr. Randy White

All rights reserved.

ISBN-13: 9781494965785
ISBN-10: 149496578X

ABSTRACT

The Affordable Health Care Act of (2010) is in the early stage of implementation as of late 2013. Commonly referred to as OBAMACARE, the health care program is designed to encourage millions of taxpayers and citizens to purchase some form of medical insurance coverage for each person including family members.

The concept of all Americans with minimum levels of medical coverage will lead to reduced insurance rates on a national basis. The premise of requiring all citizens to obtain health insurance coverage is designed to have all taxpayers pay a portion for their own medical coverage. In doing so, the concept should drive down health insurance cost associated with the indigent.

As of this writings, the insurance markets are faced with compliance issues in meeting new specific regulation related to individual and group policies. Some of these changes can be seen with no pre-existing conditions for individuals or no annual or lifetime caps on essential health benefits. The insurance underwriters are faced with cancelling of policies and reissuing policies that comply with the Affordable Health Care Act of 2010.

From a human relations perspective this process of the program intervention into the 2014 marketplace has not been well received. The public in general is not seeing the anticipated health savings. From the perspective of the individual policyholder through the company with their group medical program, costs are not being lowered. The medical community is very apprehensive with the program and the hospital community, who have millions of dollars of term debt, are not secure with the program's immediate results.

What is the solution to this dilemma? Is there an alternative solution to assist in this program for continued implementation? The matter remains to be seen.

DEDICATION

This book is dedicated to the relatives of my family from the Greatest Generation. This group of individuals gave enormous personal sacrifices to the American people that in today's world allow each and every one of us the liberties to live out our life in total freedom from tyranny and full freedom of religion.

The White Families	**The Orndoff Families**
John and Flora White	Papa and Mama Orndoff
Marion and Anice White	Jake and Opel Orndoff
Carrol and Wynell White	D.M. and Marilyn Orndoff
Wilber and Linda White	Al and Bea Snyder
Zelpha White	Reynold and Ellen Sconci
Lloyd and Dottie White	Walter and Dixie Orndoff
O.K. and Twink Dean	Francis Orndoff
Eldridge and Connie White	
Ruby Mathis White	

MISSION STATEMENT

The mission statement of this book is directed toward offering an alternative medical structure designed to meet all Americans needs; now and into the future. The program revolves around private practice participation and limited to the resource groups named in Chapter 10 – the Foundation for Reform. The Foundation for Reform will guide the process for eventual presentation to the President of the United States and his executive office in passing this proposal to Congress. The OBAMACARE reform act will not progress as intended if left to the House and the Senate, as history has shown the American public that non-patrician politics has been the downfall of our American way of life for the past forty-years as evident by Medicare, social security, national debt, and a simple balanced budget.

This reform will be orchestrated by the American public who will develop MEDICARE change from each of the twelve proposed groups (identified in this book). The will of the people will be manifest in the committee participants who have a goal to produce a composite medical program for all Americans now and in the future.

The failure of Congress to implement the OBAMACARE reform with private participants in charge is the only practical approach to Medicare governance and not to allow partisan politics to interfere in the OBAMACARE plan rollout. Historically our men and women of Congress offer the public in general a collection of very bright people who cannot collectively work together is on passing legislation beneficial to the America public. Presently the financial global community is viewing America and how we deal with the MEDICARE issue.

Congress has known about these issues for over forty-years and America the great is now in the early stages of imploding and becoming a third-world country. The former Russian Czar Khrushchev once stated, "America will implode from within." MEDICARE is but one aspect at a national financial crisis, along with Social Security, and the cumulative debt of the United States of America.

There is still time to act, as the Obama administration has a plan to counter the rising cost of medical care but the plan as seen with **OBAMACARE** needs additional assistance to ensure the American people have a plan to care for all with the best medical attention regardless of the financial capacity of each individual. We the people collectively can ensure each American has ample assets into the future to afford medical coverage for this generation, as well as other generations to come. Medicare is presently on course to bankrupt this nation, and prudent, careful consideration is needed to combat the program now and into the future.

The medical process and the sure masses of participants are a complex and complicated process. Working within a model and segmenting into various pieces allows the process can be dissected and dissimulated for future study. Each of the parts when broken down and rebuilt offers solutions approach to reworking a medical program designed to reduce spiraling cost and meet the need of the American public.

Pride is a terrible trait to have, we representing We the People.
Dr. Randy White

TABLE OF CONTENTS

ABSTRACT	iii
DEDICATION	v
MISSION STATEMENT	vii
PREFACE	xi
CHAPTER 1 – THE INSURANCE UNDERWRITER	1
CHAPTER 2 – WHERE DOES MEDICARE COME INTO PLAY	3
CHAPTER 3 – COST CONTAINMENT	5
CHAPTER 4 – THE AMERICAN PUBLIC	7
CHAPTER 5 – THE FOURTH LEG TO THE HEALTH CARE CRISIS	9
CHAPTER 6 – THE FUTURE OF HEALTH COVERAGE	11
CHAPTER 7 – REVIEW OF OTHER COMPANY BENEFITS	15
CHAPTER 8 – HEALTH INSURANCE VS TEXAS AUTO INSURANCE	17
CHAPTER 9 – WHY IS OBAMACARE IS NOT WORKING	19
CHAPTER 10 – THE FOUNDATION FOR REFORM	21
CHAPTER 11 – THE SOLUTION APPROACH – CRITICAL AREAS OF REFORM	23
CHAPTER 12 – THE COMPANY DOCTOR APPROACH	29
CHAPTER 13 – THE COMMUNITY COOPERATIVE GROUP	31
CHAPTER 14 – NATIONAL COOPERATIVE GROUP	33
CHAPTER 15 – HOW TO GET ALL CITIZENS SIGNED UP	35
CHAPTER 16 – MEDICARE MODEL	37
CHAPTER 17 – WHERE DO WE GO FROM HERE	41
REFERENCES	43

PREFACE

As a concerned citizen who has often read newspapers, watched the national and local news, the present MEDICARE rollout is tainted with flaws. Historically representation by Congress for the American public is non-existent. As a businessman who tries to best describe our historical and present day Congress, descriptive terms such as greed, power, pride, and a little arrogance comes to mind. Partisan politics rule the day; the topic is irrelevant. Each party is often ran by the most senior Congressional members who have been elected term after term and this handful of individuals collectively rule the roost.

In an attempt to offer another point of view, I have decided to introduce literature directed to our MEDICARE program as to how the present structure will not work with the Affordable Health Care Act of (2010). The enormity of the healthcare program is overwhelming; but when broken down into segments with committee members who are working toward the same goal, change can take place. Give me twelve-individuals who have varied backgrounds in the target group as seen in Chapter 10; could lead to a national health program which benefits all in present terms as well as our citizens in the future.

In closing, my intent is to solve a major issue for our country and an area which all Americans should have access to the best available medical coverage at the most economical cost. All medical students should have equal access to their individual medical education and hospitals need to be constructed in support of the medical field with the latest technology has to offer.

Chapter 1
THE INSURANCE UNDERWRITER

The insurance company (underwriter) is not a 501(c) (3) entity, but a for profit entity. The scope of their corporate existence is to provide medical insurance on an individual or group coverage basis. The insurance industry is often segregated into types of insurance coverage for the eyes, teeth, and the health of the general body. This segregation process has evolved over many decades as in this author's opinion; the eyes and teeth are part of the same body. Legislative action through lobbyist and other special interest groups has allowed for this division of the human body.

Presently the medical side of the insurance industry directed toward the human body is in turmoil in meeting the rule of the law change as directed from the Affordable Health Care Act of 2010. In view of the larger health insurers, what separates one company from another is directed toward each companies underwriting department. Over the course of time every insurance company has a well-defined plan of analysis for each medical applicant. The respective process can be categorized as proprietary to their company and this single department is what often separates a successful health insurance provider as compared to a non-successful health insurance provider.

The Affordable Health Care Act of 2010 is reflective of a mandatory process issued by the rule of law. The insurance companies offer no rebuttal to the massive health care changes; but in accordance with federal regulatory law change, they must adapt or perish. This is another area of **OBAMACARE** strategy which did little to allow input from the medical insurance carriers. This participatory lapse is a major program flaw in the development of the national healthcare program.

Chapter 2
WHERE DOES MEDICARE COME INTO PLAY

The fiscal policy associated with the present and forecasted Medicare program is at or near bankruptcy. There are numerous reasons for this program to have evolved over time to a program for retirement of individuals after a lifetime of work and the paying into Medicare for several decades. There have been several faults in this program which was designed to offer medical insurance coverage to a workforce who is at the current retirement age of 65. Numerous wrongs have been committed on this program for decades not without the knowledge of our legislative branches.

A forward looking statement for Medicare shows bankruptcy in the coming years due to several areas of our social and cultural society of today. The prognosis from a medical perspective has an American which is living longer, a general population which will outlive their financial resources and a future of the aging population with other health issues of an aging population. In addition, fewer workers are now in the workforce who can contribute financially to MEDICARE.

Chapter 3
COST CONTAINMENT

From a perspective of medical change, one of the first areas of change should be viewed be with cost containment within the medical field. The Affordable Health Care Act of 2010 does not address cost. Due to this major omission the strategy behind the business plan has allowed for a program rollout which does not encompass the most significant segment of the medical program, cost. OBAMACARE is anticipating the open market process to dictate cost. This is the first major flaw of the program.

Chapter 4
THE AMERICAN PUBLIC

The American public is now in a position of not knowing the cost of insurance premiums twelve-months from now. The person with a pre-existing condition should feel much safer in knowing their prior medical history will not allow for an underwriter to turn down a person with prior medical challenges. Many an individual is unsure if their present doctor will be allowed to continue as their medical provider. Numerous challenges and uncertainties add to the present anxiety level.

These uncertainties are not being well received and the results of individuals having to set aside additional funds for future higher medical premiums detract our economic growth and consumer spending indicators. Our financial markets do not like uncertainty. The medical providers are not sure how **OBAMACARE** will affect their individual practice and the hospitals which are costly to build, costly to maintain and they rely a large portion of their operations to Medicare and Medicaid.

Uncertainty does not allow for planned growth, as the medical field is now in a holding pattern. The insurance underwriters are adapting to change; but in a reluctant manner. The triangle of the insurance underwriter, the medical profession and the general public are all in the same position of trying to figure out where each will land.

Chapter 5
THE FOURTH LEG TO THE HEALTH CARE CRISIS

Congress, with both the House of Representatives and the United States Senate have chosen to participate in the health care solutions; but, always at opposite ends of the spectrum. This continued bickering over partisan politics has almost ruined this former great nation. Bound by party affiliation, these bright minds who are elected to represent we the people, are far from representing the general population.

Issues from the point of view of our Congress should be decided on the merits of each case undertaken and not by party affiliation. As stated by the first President of the United States in his farewell speech to Congress, George Washington cited two areas of future concern; that of not trusting a foreign entity or that of the two-party system of government for the United States of America. Such wisdom from one man over 238-years ago was sound then and still sound today.

Chapter 6
THE FUTURE OF HEALTH COVERAGE

In viewing the history of health coverage, one has to go back to WWII. Prior to world WWII medical cost was an expense, but nothing to the extent of the spiraling cost associated with health coverage as seen today and over the past forty-years.

The United States government had to address the war years and the way of life as Americans were accustomed to, changed dramatically with Pearl Harbor. Congress with the support of the President of the United States petitioned the nation to enter into a state of war. Men of all ages who were healthy and willing signed up immediately. With this mass migration of men into the armed forces, the workforce was left in short supply in a time of need.

As never seen before companies associated with the manufacturer of goods and services needed by our military began the recruitment of women into the labor force. Congress passed labor rules pertaining to wage freeze in order to allow for companies to employ the necessary level of workers to produce their goods and services at then present day non-inflationary price levels.

Due to the shortage of workers and the competitive nature of companies in hiring the women workers, companies began to get creative in how to hire the female worker while staying in line with the worker pay freeze enacted by Congress. Companies began offering health care coverage as an incentive to hire female workers to their company as compared to a non-health care coverage company.

In present times, the medical industry cost has spiraled to unseen or even unheard of levels. The cost of education for a medical doctor as well as the length of time needed to train a medical professional along with medical law suits has caused medical liability insurance to increase premiums to over $100,000 per year for the highly specialized medical professionals.

With an aging workforce, and medical issues associated with longer living plus an added factor of obesity has the medical underwriters in a vulnerable position of having to increase underwriting standards to ensure all pre-existing conditions are noted and rated.

A current trend by some companies can be seen with the cash in lieu of benefits program (Lee, 2005). This program offers an incentive in the form of cash to employees who opt out of the traditional company medical insurance program. The typical plan option is formed under an IRC Section 125 plan. These funds are discretionary by employees and could actually be used as a down payment toward a car purchase or whatever the employee would like to place these funds. Thus, the start of the exit strategy from corporate governance as a solutions approach to reducing cost which has now become a financial crisis for a company's profit and loss statement. From another accounting point of view, a cost containment solution to group medical coverage is imperative.

For many companies in the near future, medical insurance for employees will not be offered as a fringe benefit. The only companies who will offer medical coverage for employees as a current fringe benefit will be the larger and more profitable companies. All fortune 500 companies, most of the oil & gas companies along with a select number of larger companies in various industries will offer medical coverage as a standard company benefit.

With the majority of companies in the United States being considered small business, the only real benefit workers in the future will get is holiday pay, some limited form of sick pay, and little other incentive other than pay levels. All companies will comply with federal mandates related to minimum pay levels, overtime compensation, holiday pay, and hours of work per day.

The smaller family owned businesses will always have some type of medical coverage plan for the family employees and a few other non-family employees. These companies when looking toward expansion will have to take into consideration all cost associated with an employee, i.e. with medical coverage, workers compensation, overtime pay and many other employee benefit costs. Under present law, a company can't offer medical coverage for the executives of the company and not offer the same benefit for all employees of the company, regardless of their job title status.

The smaller companies will began looking to outsourcing as an option to reduce fixed operational cost and in differentiation between the employee and the contractor. The IRS has tests for companies to distinguishing between employees and that of contractors. These tests try to determine:

a) Place of work.

b) Supervision of workers.

c) Materials and supplies as paid by whom.

d) Method of payment to contractors.

e) Who is the responsible party for the paying of taxes?

f) Etc., etc.

Chapter 7
REVIEW OF OTHER COMPANY BENEFITS

In review of prior company benefits, typically a company would estimate the cost of an employee based on the employee salary plus about 40%. This was a standard budgetary amount used to reflect the following areas of company cost:

a) Salary

b) Overtime

c) Commission

d) Bonus

e) Medical insurance coverage

f) Social security and Medicare taxes

g) State unemployment taxes

h) Worker compensation

i) Retirement plans

j) Profit sharing plans

k) Employee stock option plans

l) Etc., etc.

In the mid 1980's, the company pension plan began to change. What was once customary and standard for all employees was now a non-mandatory item. The creation of the 401k was the beginning of the demise of pension plans in America. Corporate America began to change as the burden of employees' personal retirement was moved from the corporate set of books to the individual employee. The company depending upon their size and financial performance would offer a matching program with all employees up to a federal mandated limit for annual income tax deferral.

Thus, the hidden demise of the company pension plan began with the emergence of the 401k retirement plan. In my opinion, many in the workforce didn't understand how this process would affect their retirement years until they were in their sixties and they were not in position to combat the retirement issue. Corporate America in today's world has little value for the older worker with his or her expertise and often during times of industry downturns now offers standard retirement packages in efforts to reduce the workforce.

The result of the company pension movement to the 401k has altered the quality of life for retirees; as well as the age of potential retirees. The companies of the world are now seeing an aged workforce of necessity. Many a retirees is part of the voluntary workforce reduction movement as often the result of specified industry downturns. Many of these retirees often take the incentive package for retirement out of fear of being laid off without financial compensation.

In the early 1970's a retiree could take a pension of less money per month and could live within their means when their homestead was paid in full and with no debt. In today's world, a person to maintain their standard of living will often require a retirement of $4,000 per month.

What has happened over the past forty-years is the result of inflationary times which has caused the $700 per month retiree not being able to exist. The *Golden Years* for many may be a myth.

Chapter 8

HEALTH INSURANCE VS TEXAS AUTO INSURANCE

The State of Texas in working to reform automotive coverage has allowed all insured drivers to obtain optional personal-insurance-protection (PIP). This optional coverage allows the car owner to insure against the uninsured driver.

The concept was to offer full coverage to all insured in Texas in the event the insured driver was involved in an accident, at no fault of their own, with an uninsured motorist. The cost associated with the uninsured motorist was being paid for by the insured motorist group. This cost for non-participants was absorbed by others.

Similar to the Texas auto insurance challenge, the medical program referred to as OBAMACARE attempts to have all individuals participate in a health insurance program with limit amounts of coverage. The concept is to bring all participants into the program with lower contributory amounts, thus to bring more dollars to into the insurance company funds in form of premiums collectively. The anticipated results might reduce medical premiums for all.

The anticipated results from the perspective of the insurance company are not happening, with lower insurance premiums across the board. We are now seeing individual insurance health policies being cancelled or premiums on the rise or the ability of an insured to choose his or her medical provider not available. Public opinion directed towards OBAMACARE is in a mild uproar for most of America, as the larger companies with the more exclusive insurance policies are satisfied with change.

Why this happening and what is can Congress or the public do to combat or alter the present rule of law?

Chapter 9
WHY IS OBAMACARE IS NOT WORKING

There are several areas of conflict which need to be addressed prior to the OBAMACARE plan rollout. These conflicting areas were never addressed, but if these areas were to be addressed in reform of OBAMACARE, the health care program could offer an implementation plan that would address the real issues and the pending results could offer the public a plan to ensure all with wide public acceptance.

The strategists' behind OBAMACARE is not seeing the early results they anticipated. In fact, the total opposite results is now coming in with the health care rollout. There are several areas of issue with the public, the insurance carriers, the medical practitioners and the companies who provide medical insurance. With so many participants in the program all in disarray, simple economics come into play. The markets do not like the unexpected and the results of the rollout of OBAMACARE are vividly apparent.

The first major issue of why OBAMACARE is not working can be directed to Congress in being clearly divided with the program. Current day politics requires representatives to be associated with one or the other party. Secondly, the rollout party (Democrats) has approved a program that is totally opposite as to what the other party demands (Republican).

Both the House and Senate are clearly divided by party lines and the resulting legislation is impaired with this concept. Congress as a whole is elected to represent their respective constituents; but, upon arriving in Washington D.C.; their loyalty often lies within party affiliations. This in itself is the root of the problem. Until Congress can come together to resolve issues in a participatory manner, the bulk of legislation will not be in the best interest of the public in general. For this very reason, the term limits might offer the general public better representation in lieu of the present political format.

Chapter 10
THE FOUNDATION FOR REFORM

OBAMACARE is now the law of the land. We can offer areas of correction which might allow the health care program to move forward, but in an orderly and systematic manner. Healthcare in the greatest nation in the world is a right, but even a constitutional amendment has cost associated with implementation for all.

OBAMACARE as a concept is viable, but specific basic areas of the plan were never viewed or various reasons. The Affordable Health Care Act 2010 needs to address the following areas in order to create a true national healthcare reform plan. The following listing of participants to address reform could come from the following:

a) A council from the American Medical Association.

b) A council from the National Association of Insurance Carriers.

c) A council from the American Hospital Association.

d) A council from the Business Round Table.

e) A composite committee from both the House and Senate.

f) The President's Executive Office (acting as Chair) through the National Cooperative office to be located in Washington, D.C.

g) The Director of Medicare.

h) The Office of Management and Budget.

i) A council from the medical schools in the USA.

j) The American Bar Association.

k) The American Pharmaceutical Association.

l) The National Association of Realtors.

From this association of interested parties, pending legislation could eventually give rise to progressive reform of the present OBAMACARE program. Such a program would take approximately one-year; but the results from the consensus of this health reform committee might offer a total solutions approach, thereby offering the general public the best medical coverage for the least amount of money.

This proposed group of OBAMACARE reform committee would represent the majority of stakeholders involved in the process of defining and determination of a more clear and acceptable plan for OBAMACARE. The concept of a health program to insure all Americans is a prerequisite which is greatly needed and one to ensure the spiraling cost of medicine is contained in a manner to encourage continued research, medical education, and patient care.

Chapter 11

THE SOLUTION APPROACH — CRITICAL AREAS OF REFORM

In review of the present rule of law pertaining to OBAMACARE, there are several areas of concern which the reform committee will need to address and to address each of these areas in a non-political arena. If the reform committee can work on these specific issues of governance, then the American public has an opportunity to participate in a united health care program designed to offer complete medical coverage to the benefit of all Americans in healthcare plans that are practical and economically feasible from the perspective of the family budget.

The following areas will need to be addressed and in the process a majority of the current problems associated within the industry could be addressed:

a) Medical cost.

b) Hospital cost.

c) Medical education cost.

d) Medical liability insurance cost.

e) Medical software program.

f) Medical LLP or other structure assistance.

Over the course of forty-plus years there have been no concerted collective efforts to curtail spiraling medical cost associated with medical practitioners, hospital operation cost, pharmacy cost, or extended care facilities for the terminally ill. Due to these conditions, all cost associated with the medical industry is typically available only to the more financially sound Americans.

a) MEDICAL COST

Our Medicare system has also evolved with agreed to services for literally thousands of medical procedures with all medical practitioners who elect to work within the Medicare field. As a base principle, the most expedient process to control cost associated with doctors, hospitals, long term care facilities and prescriptions could be the use of the present day pricing for each of these affiliates associated within the Medicare field.

This one principle would automatically stop the frivolous billing now seen from all practitioners in the medical field, as the agreed to services for all doctors and hospitals would be based upon the current pricing scheme used nationally by Medicare. If a hospital, a practitioner group or a hospital elects to opt out of the Medicare program; so be it.

Future pricing would be controlled by Medicare and the pricing schematic would be annually reviewed for either increase or decrease in pricing based upon the consumer pricing index or another composite index that tracks inflation as well as deflationary times.

b) HOSPITAL COST

The cost to construct, staff and operate a hospital is very exorbitant in terms of present day pricing. Hospitals over the past forty-years are looking for numerous ways to cut costs and reduce the average hospital stay per patient. This process at times has been directed by Medicare and the process of telling a patient you have to be released due to Medicare limits is unacceptable. This practice is in direct conflict with that of the medical practitioner who should have the final word as to when a patient should be released.

OBAMACARE could offer an alternative solution to this release program by developing a program of financial support for all present day and future hospitals. This process could be accomplished through a program of direct compensation paid to the non-profit hospital based upon a formula to be determined by total hospital bed capacity and total bed usage with incentives for average patient stay. The hospital patient stay would be controlled by the medical practitioner as to avoid biased numbers developed by the hospital.

c) MEDICAL EDUCATION COST

The cost and time for a medical student to become a licensed medical practitioner now covers several hundred thousands of dollars and several years. Upon the completion of the education process, the typical student might have incurred debt of several hundred thousands of dollars personally.

This process could be addressed collectively by a council from the medical schools as a committee to address alternatives to the high rising cost of medical school tuition, books, labs, along with room and board. By addressing the issue by the universities of medical study providers, this one method might offer several solutions to the spiraling cost and offer other support areas for the students who wish to obtain the medical diploma in all fields of medicine.

One solution to the rising cost could be seen with the building of special dorms directed toward the medical students or similar to the dorms now provided to athletics. The capital cost is one item, but when viewed over the course of forty-years the price for housing on campus could be drastically reduced when compared to present day commercial housing used around the country today.

Secondly, the medical schools might look into the freezing of tuition rates with the support of some type of inflationary based index directed to accessing inflation or deflationary periods of time. This index table could be used with a pricing support from Medicare as a process designed to encourage students into the medical field with a base level of support for housing along with room and board paid direct to the participating university.

Thirdly, another area to reduce time in the educational process might allow medical students to be released from classes which often amount to elective classes that are not directed to the medical field. This process could reduce the medical education by one year with the dropping of elective courses. Often medical students' elective courses are typically classes which require little study and have no direct bearing on their medical degree.

Students who have the passion, drive, and grades to work through the educational process could be the winners at graduation time, with small amounts of debt with a subsided medical education program. This program is just one of the pieces of the puzzle in addressing higher and higher cost associated with the process of becoming a licensed doctor within the United States.

d) MEDICAL LIABLITY INSURANCE COST

The cost of liability insurance associated with the medical field is spiraling out of control. The field of medical liability insurance is often underwritten dependent upon the type of practice as when one compares the general practitioner to that of a heart surgeon; the premiums begin to escalate to six-figure portions. This is totally unacceptable and the premiums are reflective of the underwriting and the insurance companies' historical data associated with medical settlements and insurance company payouts.

Tort reform is needed over a national level. The present day American Bar Association could offer solutions to these spiraling jury awards with legislation directed toward the injured patient and his or hers historical earnings and future earnings. There have been several trails by juries who have issued punitive and actual damages of millions of dollars to a person who has a history of low wage. This is but one method that might be used to determine damages and awards.

A second method to review could be based upon the future cost of care for an injured patient over their estimated length of life. This method would rely upon the practitioner prognosis and current cost associated with patient care, therapy, and other medical care that will needed to be provided into the future.

These are but two example of placing a dollar figure on patient damages for the present and into the future. Many a person will find this process totally grotesque, inhumane and not a responsive approach to placing a dollar value toward future care. Keep in mind how often does a multi-million dollar tax free insurance award go not to the benefit of the injured party, but to other family members who used the position of custodian to purchase homes, cars, vacations and almost any area other than the direct care of the patient.

Again, this is but one piece to the total composite puzzle of medical cost with the scope of attempting to care for all with the best possible medical advice to the total aging population as a whole. For **OBAMACARE** to evolve, each of these areas must be addressed to ensure there are future funds to cover from our present day grandchildren and their children. Presently **MEDICARE** is on course to bankrupt this great nation and **MEDICARE** along with the interest on accelerating debt of the United States could alter the current status of our country from the world leader, to that of a third-world country.

e) MEDICAL SOFTWARE PROGRAM

As of this writing the software plan to rollout **OBAMACARE** will not be fully operational till late 2014. Due to this present condition, the timing is available to collectively work toward reform. This reform will require all stakeholders to participate in committee form and each chair of each committee with have their specific mission statement along with a scope of their specific committee work while working within a time frame sequence.

Presently the software delays are associated with the sheer capacity of the project, but of all of the areas of concern, the software solution is the most finite to produce results. The sheer numbers of 50,000 online users at any one time takes an enormous amount of time and computer capacity to accomplish this task. The real risk with the software program is minimal with time being the real problem, as the technology and personnel know how is in ample supply.

The capital cost associated with the administration of OBAMACARE has now been covered, as the country awaits each segment of the program to be opened up in the coming months. The ongoing cost of the software program and personnel will be budged by MEDICARE.

f) MEDICAL LLP AND OTHER STRUCTURES ASSISTANCE

In an effort to assist the medical practitioners in their individual efforts to revamp their private practices, the American Bar Association and the National Association of Realtors could offer a solutions approach to assist the medical field with their current legal structures. These legal structures often have attached leases for their office and medical clinics and the union of these two national associations might be able to offer a solutions approach to assist the various medical groups in either a merger or office relation with a merger.

Concerted effort of the dozen listed national associations could offer a total solutions approach to assist with the rollout of OBAMACARE. The pending results of these various committees are designed to reduce the cost of medical access to the average person in the United States.

The anticipated results of this process might place a sole practitioner in a position of receiving less monthly funding which would in turn damage the sole practitioner from a financial standpoint. If this were to be the case, the retro fitting of OBAMACARE would allow a sole practitioner to join his or her practice with another group of cooperative participating doctors. This program would offer the doctor the ability to terminate or expand his or her practice without having to go through the legal system to obtain this process.

Chapter 12
THE COMPANY DOCTOR APPROACH

During the post war years of WWII, America began the process of turning away from the war production years to that of the nation's economic resurgence. With millions of our military personnel returning back to civilian life, change was evident. The face of the American workforce changed; women went from the breadwinner role back to that of the household and the role of raising their family.

Companies began to grow and prosper as America would continue to grow in their role as the global provider for financial, manufacturing and production and technology efforts. Corporate America began to expand as never seen before and during this process medical care for their respective employees helped to usher in the company doctor program. In the 1950s and 1960s, it was not uncommon for a company employee to travel to various locations of company sites. Each company location had what they often referred to as a company doctor. When a visiting employee would travel into a new region and the employee required some form of medical assistance; the employee would often use this process for his or her medical needs.

This whole process was established to allow employee travel between locations that required medical assistance with a program designed to be cost effective and expedient.

The doctor's office often billed the company either a flat rate fee or a monthly statement based upon patient visits from the company. This company doctor concept was designed to control medical cost for all traveling company personnel for the mutual benefit of the company in having a healthy workforce within a cost containment program.

This process has evolved to allow companies the ability to offer all of their employees' access to the best possible medicine, medical facilities and medical practitioners at the lowest possible cost to the company. This modern day approach can be seen with the NASA-JSC contract with the Kelsey-Seybold Clinics. This model represents a benchmark approach to reducing historical rising medical cost by allowing companies to pay direct a stated fee to the providers for each participant within their plan; no matter or not, if the participants use the medical practitioners services. This model places the cost containment program the responsibility to the medical provider or in this specific case, Kelsey-Seybold Clinics.

Kelsey-Seybold Clinics in their contract with NASA-JSC have a "medical practitioner group of over 400 occupational medicine and environmental health professionals across 10 primary NASA Centers" (2000, Campion). This concept allows for both the company and the cooperative medical group to work together in providing both preventative and at need medical services directed to reducing medical cost presently and into the future. This benchmark is a model that OBAMACARE needs to emulate as the program works.

The Kelsey-Seybold Clinical approach is designed to give more control back to the individual doctor when dealing one-on-one with the patient. Under this structure, the medical practitioner will determine the type of testing required, can collaborate with other specialized within his cooperative, and can determine when the patient can leave the hospital. Under our present structure of medical practitioner and insurance company; the medical practitioner needs to be keenly aware of each insurance company and their standards of reimbursed coverage. Under the Kelsey-Seybold approach, all medical decisions are made within the confines of the cooperative. This model of medical care is designed to curb medical cost and to give the patient the best medical advice possible without the interference of the insurance company.

Chapter 13
THE COMMUNITY COOPERATIVE GROUP

Similar to the Kelsey-Seybold Clinic approach, the smaller communities in the United States can develop a similar approach to medical treatment with the company doctor approach. Each respective medical specialty within a given community could form a cooperative with Medicare and the collective group would be paid a base fee per resident of the community. The cooperative would be a collection of individual medical practitioners who each maintain their individual identity with their present form of medical care; but in their association within a local cooperative; the group could develop a revenue stream for each plan participant who resides in the area.

Each cooperative would need to partner with the local hospital or a group of area hospitals as a cooperative member to ensure all medical needs are covered for the citizens of their area.

The cooperative association would have non-profit status, as the cooperative would be charged with the disbursement of monthly Medicare funds received to each of the cooperative members. This disbursement program would develop their own plan of disbursement dependent upon some type of appropriation based on patient visits and maybe degree of care. Degree of care can be seen with a patient visit to a general practitioner for a common cold, verses that of a heart patient visit with a cardiologist. Each cooperative could develop their own program for Medicare disbursements which could be altered in the after month, dependent upon patient visits.

Even in a rural area, all practitioner participants could still maintain present form of practice while participating in a rural cooperative. If a practitioner did not want to work within the rural cooperative program, then so be it.

Another option the rural cooperatives could have is often rural communities do not have access to specialize areas of medical practice. The cooperative could develop what is known as an intra-service agreement between the cooperatives. This would be a type of transfer's agreement whereby a rural patient needing a particular type of specialist would be transferred to the urban cooperative. This agreement could provide for compensation between each cooperative or some type of credit program developed and dependent upon the degree of specialized medicine required. The regulatory agency in Washington D.C. acting as the national cooperative organization could initiate the guidelines for transfers between cooperatives.

Bear in mind, the OBAMACARE MEDICARE program as this model suggest, will still allow all medical practitioners, hospitals, and other health care support groups to still provide for non OBAMACARE programs. The larger companies in the United States will continue to offer group medical benefits to all their employees and each of the three identified areas can still participate in this private sector.

If a hospital or medical practitioner chooses not to participate in this model of OBAMACARE or the Affordable Health Care Act of (2010), then this is their prerogative.

These medical practitioners and hospitals could continue to operate using private medical insurance as they might deem necessary. Additionally, all medical practitioners, hospitals and other health care support groups could operate in both areas with revenue streams coming from MEDICARE as well as the companies that continue to offer group medical coverage for their employees.

Chapter 14
NATIONAL COOPERATIVE GROUP

From a national perspective, each cooperative would be part of a national cooperative organization out of Washington D.C. The purpose of this type of holding entity would be responsible to organize a national coverage program for all United States participants who travel within the United States and who will require medical attention when away from his or her registered cooperative. The national organization will offer structure, continuity, and act in their capacity as the regulatory branch of the national cooperative program. The national association would be controlled by a board elected by all cooperatives under 2-year terms and their budget would come from the cooperatives as a non-profit form.

The national organization would be charged with the development of a program with all countries in the world to ensure all United States citizens and cooperative participants have seamless coverage on a global basis. This process would require reciprocal government agreements between all nations or similar to the medical agreements used in Mexico with foreign United States citizens who require medical treatment while in the sovereign country of Mexico.

The national cooperative group would require strong transformational leadership with a clear understanding of the process designed to control medical cost at the cooperative level, while expanding this vision throughout the globe. The national leader would be elected on a bi-annual basis with a board of directors also elected by the cooperative with one vote per cooperative regardless of cooperative size.

The cooperative would be independent of any of the branches of our government and would operative independently of the federal government agency.

The independence of the national cooperative group is a prerequisite to sound management and finance while outside the typical role of politics and the Washington D.C. bureaucracy. The national cooperative group will be charged with the management, disbursement, oversight, and the governing body for each cooperative. The success of this program allows no regulation by any branch of our government as the agency will be independent of government oversight.

Any form of government oversight would over time kill the intent and purpose of the program as history will show all Americans that more government is not the solution to success and often a hindrance to the logic and intent of a national health care program.

Presently in the United States there are several regional cooperatives which offer total medical management. One of these medical cooperatives can be seen with the Group Health Cooperative of Washington and the Health Partners in Minnesota. These organizations have evolved over time and their evolution allows for medical cost containment to continually evolve within each cooperative.

Chapter 15

HOW TO GET ALL CITIZENS SIGNED UP

"The present system of the individual mandate requires people to carry at least a minimum level of health coverage or pay a tax proportional to their income (Nemeth, 2013). From a practical point of view, the same targeted populace not previously covered by any form of medical coverage will more than likely not participate in this national program.

To alter this risk of less than full participation, the OBAMA administration needs to put forth a concerted effort to draw attention to the health insurance mandate or a program similar to the census survey the government conducts every decade.

A program like this could offer a higher compliance rate over a one-year time period. Governmental workers on the street level could assist with the enrollment process with hand held electronic application processing to complete the application process. For OBAMACARE to perform as anticipated, full participation must be met according to the working model for the health care program.

A large portion of the population who is covered by their employer is not required to participate. This group could represent approximately 30% of the workforce while working for the larger corporations in America. The target group for OBAMACARE will be directed toward the small business section and the self-employed. The real test of this program will be directed toward this sector with many potential participants that live on the minimum wage scale and often have work related interruptions due to inclement weather conditions.

Full participant compliance within the OBAMACARE program will allow the process to work as designed. Any material deviation from this business model will not allow for adequate cash flow to support the national model. The few who do not participate will continue to operate as usual with the emergency room as their primary care provider.

Chapter 16
MEDICARE MODEL

The financial model will be based upon the average United States annual wage per worker with a percentage of each Medicare payment directed to the following model. This model is presented for presentation purposes and the actual percentage could be altered to ensure the program has perpetual existence. The model will be based upon an average annual salary of $42,000.

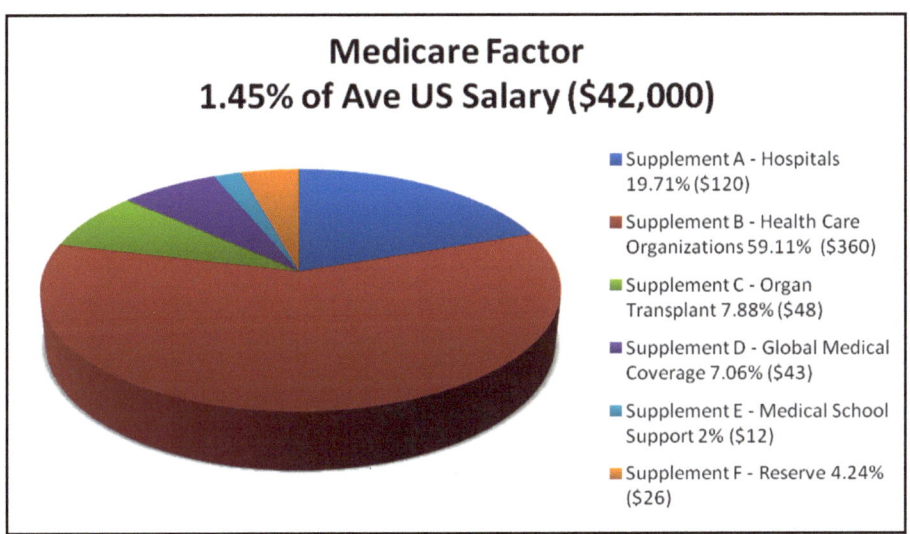

Based upon this model, Medicare is designed to payout monthly directly to all participating hospitals, health care organizations, reserve funds for organ transplants which typically run into the hundreds of thousands of dollars, with funds set aside for all plan participants who experience medical trauma while traveling outside the confirms of the United States, and finally a reserve fund to ensure the continued growth reserves for Medicare.

Supplement A – Hospitals

All participating hospitals would be paid a fixed monthly fee based upon the number of hospital beds. These fixed payments would be monitored and regulated by national organization located in Washington D.C. The participating hospitals will continue to operate in their present structure, if they elect to do so.

Supplement B – Health Care Organizations

With national coverage, health care organizations would be based on demographic areas; as both rural and urban areas would be divided and supported by cooperative associations. Based upon the cooperative area population, each cooperative would be paid a fixed fee per month for all participants, even though a participant may not utilize the service of the cooperative. This program is designed to allow the cost containment within each cooperative. The cooperative would handle all medical cases including to organ transplant, if their cooperative offers the services.

Supplement C – Organ Transplant

Due to the high cost associated with organ transplants, the national organization would budget on a monthly basis funds set aside to cover this vital type of emergency surgery. The national health care organization out of Washington D.C. will budget and monitor the program on a monthly basis to ensure ample fund reserves are maintained for the future.

Supplement D – Global Medical Coverage

The average American when away from his or her homestead for two-weeks per year correlates to a percentage away from home annually of 8%; thereby the plan participants are within their home area of 92%. Global participant travelers would be covered under a global plan with a reimbursement program for injured or ill participants. Presently the United States has government to government relationships with foreign countries which allow foreign embassies on a global basis. This present structure allows for reciprocal medical agreements to be put in place within an orderly period of time.

Supplement E – Medical School Support

With the high cost of a medical field education, the length of time for a tested and licensed medical doctor or other specialist within the medical field can take years. The national health care organization could work in close association with all participating medical schools to reduce medical educational cost and to reduce the time necessary to educate a medical field practitioner. One area of medical education time reduction can be seen in reducing the amount of electives for a typical bachelor degree. Approximately twenty-hours are electives which have little or no bearing on the medical field; these courses could be dropped thereby reducing the total number of hours need to obtain a degree for medical students.

Supplement F – Reserve

Prudent financial budgeting requires reserves. The medical model for reserve could allow for up to 4.24% of the Medicare premium paid in monthly through payroll deduction and company matching. These reserve funds should be allowed to invest in overnight governmental securities such as T-bills with the interest earned coming back into the trust account on a daily basis. This process in effect would allow for compounding of the reserve fund.

Chapter 17
WHERE DO WE GO FROM HERE

The history of America is like no other in the world. This country is relatively young in terms of age in comparison to the other countries in the world. The United States of America is a world leader in almost all categories of medicine, education, finance, knowledge and all offered under the auspices of free enterprises. Our system of governance allows for prosperity and growth to those who strive for excellence. In no other country in the world does one have the ability to prosper; as evident by the United States having to limit immigration access to our country each and every year.

The Obama Administration needs to assimilate an OBAMACARE reform committee to begin the process of building the twelve areas of committee members as directed in Chapter 10 - THE FOUNDATION FOR REFORM. This initial process would offer the beginnings of the committee to address the major issues in offering reform to the present OBAMACARE program.

As previously mentioned, OBAMACARE program is a workable and a much needed medical program; but, under the program present status, the program falls short of addressing cost associated within the medical field. Please see CHAPTER 11 for itemized areas of cost.

These twelve committee heads represent the American hope of reform and a reformation which could be complete within twelve-months of enactment. The reformation could coincide with the completion of the OBAMACARE website which should be fully functional by the year 2015. The completion of this committee would be a milestone and a benchmark for review by both the House and Senate in how people of different backgrounds could come together for a common cause and to offer a total solutions approach without pork in meeting the needs of all Americans; without the shame of present Congressional leaders bickering while not making decisions for the benefit of the American public in general.

REFERENCES

Campion, E. (2010). *NASA-JSC awards contract to Kelsey-Seybold Clinic.* Retrieved from http://www.nasa.gov/centers/johnson/news/releases/1999_2001/j00-40.txt

Lee, J. (2010). *Cash in lieu of benefits.* Retrieved from http://www.johnsondugan.blogs.com/ main/2005/07/cash_in_lieu_of.html

Nemeth, N. (2013). IRS works to clarify the Affordable Care Act's individual mandate. *The IRS Relief Newsletter, 20*(27), 1.

www.ingramcontent.com/pod-product-compliance
Lightning Source LLC
Chambersburg PA
CBHW040901180526
45159CB00001B/486